MY *Mindful* JOURNEY

IN THE MIDST OF THINGS, REMEMBER YOU CAN STILL SHINE WHERE YOU ARE.

WHAT IS *Mindfulness*?

The Practice of mindfulness is one of the simplest things you can do for your wellbeing. It is something that individuals from all walks of life can benefit from. You can do it anywhere at any time.

Mindfulness is the quality of being present on purpose and fully engaged maintaining a moment-by-moment awareness of our thoughts, feelings, bodily sensations, and surrounding environment, through a gentle, nurturing lens. When we practice mindfulness, our thoughts tune into what we're sensing in the present moment rather than rehashing the past or imagining the future.

FOUR FOUNDATIONS OF *Mindfulness*

- Mindfulness of the body.
- Mindfulness of feelings.
- Mindfulness of mind.
- Mindfulness of Dhamma.

THREE KEY COMPONENTS OF *Mindfulness*

Attention, Intention, Attitude.

Mindful In the midst

TO BE *Mindful* IN THE MIDST

CAN YOU BE BOTH?

"It might seem crazy to want to be more conscious of illness and discomfort. Yet mindful — moment to moment, nonjudgmental awareness — may be exactly what your body most needs when you are run down and under the weather. Says Mark Bertin, M.D specializes in developmental pediatrics."

Growing up, I was unaware of so many things in regards to my health. I knew that I had sickle cell disease and that it was painful. My first pain crisis was at the age of 6.

What I didn't know was that one fall would lead me to multiple hospital visits for the rest of my life. At least that's what I thought started my hospital visits. I thought because I fell out of the chair, I was sick.

I later realized it wasn't because of the fall and that I had a chronic illness. No one ever told me that chronic meant constantly recurring. So, therefore, I spent a lot of time alone without family because my parents were not able to spend weeks in the hospital with me.

As for any parent, it was hard seeing their child laying there helpless. My mother gave me tools to use as I laid in the hospital. I was unaware of the tools I was being taught to use every time I did not feel well.

When I got older, I would suggest that people use mindfulness to help manage pain. I didn't realize what I was taught was considered another form of meditation for pain management. Through mindfulness and meditation, I learned how to help manage my physical and mental health.

It helped, but it did not take the place of seeing a doctor. Through mindful practices and meditation, I developed a state of mental immunity. It helped me to have a healthy outlook and to maintain my peace and joy over the years.

Being born with a chronic condition, stress, and anything weighing heavy on my life, can send me straight to the ER. Therefore, I have to be very careful of the thoughts and things that I let into my mind. I don't allow anyone to steal or harm my joy.

My experience helped me to understand that building my mental immunity keeps my mind at peace even when I have my regular sickle cell crisis. Yes, I get angry, and yes, I have negative thoughts and emotions. I am human.

I grew up preparing and building my mind to fight this disease, so I built this level of joy and peace I have in my life. I understand how much work, time, and consistency it takes to live a joyful and positive life despite everything. My goal is to be the voice that inspires others to start their journey to live a healthier, positive, and inspired life.

So, yes, you can be mindful in the midst.

tayo togba

— Tayo Togba, Certified Mindfulness Practitioner

Mindfulness + PAIN MANAGEMENT

There is increasing evidence that regular mindfulness practice reduces a person's pain experience. Pain is a complex experience. What you feel isn't exactly the same as what someone else feels. Pain almost always has emotional and psychological components (in addition to physical pain), there is no objective test that can quantify the exact degree of pain a person is feeling. One thing that is definite, we all know pain when we feel it.

Mindfulness is not like traditional painkillers, which are intended to dull or eliminate pain. The goal of mindful practices is typically not to remove pain entirely, but to change your relationship with it so that you are able to experience relief and healing in the middle of uncomfortable physical sensations.

Mindfulness can also help you create a more flexible sense of self. Pain impacts a person's identity. By practicing mindfulness you understand pain is a physical sensation, not your identity. You are a whole human being who is dealing with a medical condition. By learning to be mindful, you can observe pain with a stable, compassionate, and curious mind. With systemic pain that does have a cause, mindfulness helps people cope with it better. You can identify pain sensations and your physical, mental and emotional reactions to pain sensations. By training your mind to be in the present moment, it helps you put your energy into skillful choices in living well today. That allows you to approach your pain with less fear and more acceptance. Allowing you to live life fully, even though you have pain.

Mindful In the midst

Mindful MEDITATION

Meditation offers time for relaxation and heightened awareness in a stressful world where our senses are dulled. Research suggests that meditation has the potential for more than just temporary stress relief. Educators, spiritual leaders, and mental health experts have developed dozens of forms of meditation. The variety suggests there is a form of meditation to suit most people, regardless of personality or lifestyle. For someone who meditates, the practice offers a chance to improve physical wellbeing, as well as emotional health. However, there is no "right way" to meditate, meaning people can explore the different types until they find one that works for them.

THERE ARE SEVEN *meditations*

1. Loving-kindness meditation
2. Body scan or progressive relaxation
3. Mindfulness meditation
4. Breath awareness meditation
5. Kundalini yoga
6. Zen meditation
7. Transcendental Meditation

Mindful In the midst

THE BENEFITS OF *Mindfulness*

Mindfulness is an incredible tool to help people understand, tolerate, and deal with their emotions in healthy ways. Research demonstrates that mindfulness bolsters our immune system, help manage chronic pain, reduces anxiety, improves attention, and banishes temporary negative feelings. People who incorporate mindfulness into their lives often report heightened levels of happiness, patience, acceptance, and compassion. It helps us to alter our habitual responses by taking pause and choosing how we act. Mindfulness purposely brings one's attention to experiences occurring in the present moment without judgment. It provides pragmatic principles and practical techniques to overcome negative thoughts and feelings, in a way that is lasting, sustainable, and healthy for your well being.

THE BENEFITS OF *journaling*

Allows time to self reflect.
Reduces Stress.
Improves Immune Function.
Keeps Memory Sharp.
Boosts Mood.

Mindful In the midst

LETTER TO *Myself*

I understand that mindfulness is

FILL IN THE BLANK

I am aware that this journal is for my personal well-being. Every time I open this journal I know that I will sometimes be in a hard place. I know that my emotions will possibly run rapidly, but I will continue to write. I know that every time I open my journal I am opening it for a reason, and that reason is a part of my personal journey. I know that no matter how hard it gets to write I will continue to put my pen to paper every chance I get. In the midst of me being where I am, when I open this journal I understand that I will be opening a new part of my life up to myself with every journal entry.

SIGNATURE

Mindful **In the midst**

Mindful WRITING

Keeping a journal is good for you — physically, mentally, and emotionally... but what if, like many of us, you find yourself stuck, staring fruitlessly at a blank page? This Journal has mindful writing prompts to help guide you through many emotions that happens in a health facility. It offer you an idea of what to write about from moment to moment.

WRITING Motivation

Writing by hand stimulates and trains the brain in a way digital communication doesn't.

- Don't censor yourself. Let it all go.
- Don't preoccupy yourself with managing perfect punctuation, grammar, or spelling.
- Write as much or as little as you want.
- Start writing and keep your pen moving until there's a natural pause and you feel finished with that train of thought.
- Honoring all of your feelings is how you empower the feelings you want to generate more of.
- Write notes as you recall an experience.

Mindful **In the midst**

Mindful WRITING PROMPTS

1) Wellbeing

My wait time is...
In this moment I feel...
I am being asked many questions...
I feel sleep deprived...
I refused...
I am being discharged...
I am being prematurely discharged..
They are giving me...
No one came to visit me...
I had visitors...
My pain level at this moment...
How were you affected emotionally...

2) Connect

The communication is clear and concise...
There is a lack of clear communication...
The staff member tone of voice...
My tone of voice is...
My physician is not available...
My physician is available...
I am being treated well...
I am not being treated well...
I had a great dialogue with the staff...
I had a bad dialogue with the staff...
I understand my treatment plan...
I do not understand my treatment plan...
How were your interactions with the doctor and office staff?
My advocate helps me...

3) Healing

The feelings I am experiencing at this moment...
The things that help me the most right now...
The things that help me the least right now...
If I were to adopt a new way of seeing this moment..
What are some affirmations I could say right now to affirm my desired feelings right now...
At this moment I feel...
I feel strong when...
I feel weak when...
I need right now in this present moment?
Where can I be more receptive or open at this moment?
If I am not happy at this moment, I know that it's okay to feel this way.
What is in my power in this moment to change that?
Some things I could stop doing so I could better align with how I want to feel at this moment...
The next time I experience a negative emotion, I am going to...
Some ways I could honor negative emotions without judgment are...

Mindful In the midst

Mindful WRITING PROMPTS

(4) Gratitude

I am grateful for...
How can I practice gratitude at this moment?
Are there areas in which I am privileged and thus, have gratitude?
What are three things I am thankful for right now, in this very instance?
Among the things I need, which do I have?
Among the things I do not need, which do I have?
Is there a thing/person/situation that you're grateful for every day...
Have or are you experiencing an obstacle now and want to overcome it in the future? Be already grateful for that.

(5) Self-Care

What does self-care look like to me...
What can I do in this moment as a form of self-care?
What are the things I am already doing for self-care?
What is stopping me from taking care of myself?
I am being kind to myself by...
I am being kind to others by...
What makes me relaxed?
What are the things that consume most of my time and energy?
Self-care to-do list...
Bad day checklist...
I advocate for myself by...
Eating habits...
Water log...

(6) Reflection

Write a short story of your visit.
If the story is negative rewrite the story how you envisioned it should have gone.
If the story was positive. Write things that you can do to make more of your visits that way...
What I know now...
What is the most frustrating part of your pain...
What is the most frustrating part of your illness...
What challenge I had that turned out to be a gift in disguise (even if it's still painful)? Why?
How might this experience transform me into a more loving (compassionate, forgiving, patient, helpful, or faithful) person?
Was it a positive or negative impact...
What positive thing have I learned about myself...
What negative thing have I learned about myself...
This caused me...
What does my life feel like right now?
This visit made me feel...

Mindful In the midst

S.

mission.

"Find Your Shine Where You Are" is more than a mission; it's a movement to inspire and uplift individuals on their path to self-discovery, empowerment, and positive impact, right from their current place in life.

about.

At "Find Your Shine Where You Are," our mission is to inspire, empower, and support individuals in discovering their inner light, fostering personal growth, and making a positive impact on their communities. We believe that everyone possesses a unique brilliance, and it is our purpose to help them uncover it right where they are.

defining my shine.

Begin by defining what "shining" means to you in the context of self-development. Write a personal mission statement that encapsulates your goals and aspirations.

shine through challenges.

Document a day dedicated to self-care. Describe the self-care activities you engaged in and how they made you shine from the inside out.

1. mindful shine stroll.

Practice mindfulness during your walk. Pay attention to the sights, sounds, and sensations around you. Notice how your body and mind can shine when you are fully present.

2. sunrise shine walk.

Schedule a walk during sunrise to witness the world coming to life. As you walk, embrace the warmth of the sun and visualize it infusing you with energy and positivity.

3. shine + stretch.

Dedicate time each day to indoor stretching exercises. Stretching can help increase flexibility and reduce muscle tension, allowing you to shine in your daily life.

4. shine through artistry.

Explore your creative side with an art project indoors. Whether it's painting, crafting, or writing, engage in activities that let your inner light shine through your artistic expressions.

5. shine with music.

Create a playlist of your favorite uplifting songs or soothing melodies. Music can have a profound impact on your mood and help you shine.

6. shine in new habits.

Describe new habits you're cultivating to promote self-development. Explore how these habits are shaping your character and helping you shine.

7. shine path of gratitude.

As you walk, list three things you are grateful for. Recognize how gratitude can help you shine brighter, even on difficult days.

8. shine through challenges.

Schedule a walk during sunrise to witness the world coming to life. As you walk, embrace the warmth of the sun and visualize it infusing you with energy and positivity.

9. shine in silence.

Dedicate a portion of your walk to silence. Use this time to connect with your inner self, focus on your breathing, and allow your inner light to shine through the quiet moments.

10. shine acts of kindness.

Plan small acts of kindness that you can perform from where you are, such as writing a heartfelt letter or sending an encouraging message to someone who may need it.

11. hydrate and shine.

Stay well-hydrated to keep your skin looking and feeling healthy. Proper hydration allows your inner beauty to shine through.

12. shine support.

Reach out to a friend, family member, or support group to discuss your journey and the progress you've made. Share your insights and ask for their support and feedback.

SHINE THROUGH YOUR JOURNALING PRACTICE

BUT FIND YOUR SHINE WHERE YOU ARE.

Made in the USA
Columbia, SC
01 July 2024

10748e0d-7f0c-4a29-8e1e-dc8540921adaR01